MINDFULNESS
— FOR —
EVERY DAY
JOURNAL

Simple Tips and Guided Exercises
to Help You Live in the Moment

MINDFULNESS FOR EVERY DAY JOURNAL

This fully updated and revised edition copyright © Summersdale Publishers Ltd, 2023
First published as *The Little Book of Mindfulness* in 2019
Published as *Mindfulness for Every Day* in 2022

Text by Gilly Pickup, updated and revised by Holly Brook-Piper

An Hachette UK Company
www.hachette.co.uk

Vie Books, an imprint of Summersdale Publishers Ltd
Part of Octopus Publishing Group Limited
Carmelite House
50 Victoria Embankment
LONDON
EC4Y 0DZ
UK

www.summersdale.com

Printed and bound in the Czech Republic

ISBN: 978-1-80007-835-2

Substantial discounts on bulk quantities of Summersdale books are available to corporations, professional associations and other organizations. For details contact general enquiries: telephone: +44 (0) 1243 771107 or email: enquiries@summersdale.com.

This journal belongs to:

....

Date of birth:

....

Date:

....

How I feel before embarking on this journey:

....

....

Completion date:

....

How I feel now I have completed this journey:

....

....

INTRODUCTION

You may have chosen this book because you want to feel less stressed, improve your quality of life or increase your focus. Whatever your motive, there is no doubt that practising mindfulness is one of the easiest and most effective solutions to bettering your life in many areas. Full of tips, advice, inspirational journal prompts and thoughtful quotes to help you embrace the power of the present moment, this book delivers all you need to make every day one of appreciation and peace.

HOW TO USE THIS JOURNAL

Mindfulness works like a muscle; the more you exercise it, the stronger it gets. Journaling will be most effective if you do it regularly, so try to find a few moments to work through the prompts on the following pages every day. By making it a habit, you will discover mindfulness becomes a way of life instead of something you struggle to maintain. Be as detailed in your writing as you can; the more detailed your writing is, the greater the insight you will have into your thoughts, feelings and future.

Lastly, don't let anything hold you back – there is no right or wrong to what you write in this journal, it is yours alone so be honest with yourself and try not to censor your writing.

MINDFULNESS EXPLAINED

What exactly is mindfulness? Also known as present moment awareness, in simple terms, mindfulness is about focusing on the present moment. The practice of mindfulness dates back thousands of years, with its roots deeply engrained in Eastern religions and traditions, such as Hinduism and Buddhism. It is the practice of being fully aware of where you are and what you are doing, without becoming overwhelmed by everything that is happening around you. This is achieved by being totally conscious of your surroundings, emotions and thoughts, while concentrating your attention on whatever is happening in the here and now. You might ask yourself, how will mindfulness benefit me? For one thing, it can help banish those niggling feelings of anxiety and tension that sometimes come along and threaten your peace of mind. Living mindfully brings many other rewards, including improved mood and strengthened mental health.

Use the space below to answer the following questions:

What does mindfulness mean to you?

....

....

....

What do you want to achieve through mindfulness?

....

....

....

What life goals do you want to accomplish with the help of mindfulness?

....

....

....

How will accomplishing these goals positively benefit your life?

....

....

....

Use this space to write your own thoughts.

NO DISTRACTIONS

When you first start to practise mindfulness, eliminate distractions. Choose a peaceful space, switch off your phone and cut out as much external noise as possible. Focus on your breathing. Notice how each breath moves in and out of your body. If your mind starts to wander, bring your focus back to your breathing. The more you focus, the easier it gets. If you notice that you're thinking ahead to what you're going to do next, gently nudge your attention back to the present. Although mindfulness is all about paying attention to what's happening around you right now, it doesn't mean shutting out every thought you have. Your mind doesn't come with an "off" switch. It is about dealing more creatively with those thoughts and experiencing life as it unfolds, moment by moment.

**Use the space below to answer
the following questions:**

In the past, what has held you back from starting your
mindfulness journey? How have you overcome this?

....

....

....

How often would you like to practise mindfulness? Set
yourself a mindfulness aim – even if it's five minutes a day.

....

....

....

....

....

Reflect upon the reasons why you deserve
time for self-care and reflection.

....

....

....

....

....

....

Use this space to write your own thoughts.

MINDFULNESS ISN'T DIFFICULT; WE JUST NEED TO REMEMBER TO DO IT.

Sharon Salzberg

ANYTIME, ANYWHERE

One of the great things about mindfulness is that you can practise it wherever you are. You don't even need to set aside a special time because you can be mindful of your surroundings at any moment in your day. While out walking, for example, or when you are in the gym, making dinner or relaxing. All you have to do is focus your attention on your body, thoughts, emotions or the surrounding environment. Of course, developing a daily mindfulness practice takes patience and determination. It can be hard work to keep pulling your mind back to the present moment. One of the easiest ways to do this is to breathe slowly and deeply. Stay with it. As you become more familiar with the practice, benefits will become more obvious. You will start to feel more present, peaceful and alive. Remember, mindfulness works like a muscle: the more you exercise it, the stronger it gets.

Consider times in your day when you can practise mindfulness. It doesn't have to be when you are sat alone in a quiet room, it can be as you wait for the kettle to boil or standing in a queue.

Morning

....

....

....

Afternoon

....

....

....

Evening

....

....

....

When have you found is the most effective time for you to practise mindfulness?

....

....

....

Use this space to write your own thoughts.

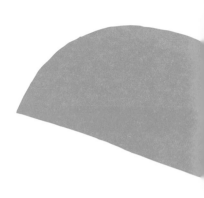

FOCUS ON THE HERE AND NOW

Try not to compare the past with the present.
If you find your mind is drifting while you are
having a mindful moment, make your thoughts
home in on what's good now by thinking of
one thing that you are grateful for. It needn't
be anything huge; it could simply be that
you are grateful that the sun is shining or
appreciating your morning cup of tea or coffee.

Today I am grateful for:

1. ....

2. ....

3. ....

4. ....

5. ....

In the space below, write down any ways you can think of to show your gratitude.

....

....

....

....

....

....

....

....

How does being grateful make you feel?

....

....

Use this space to write your own thoughts.

I LOVE
AND ACCEPT
MYSELF JUST
AS I AM

UNDERSTAND YOURSELF

Mindfulness enables you to be more aware of your body and is the key to understanding yourself. The body is an amazing, complex machine but it can be easy to forget to show our true appreciation and take it for granted. Mindfulness can help you re-engage with your physical self and by appreciating all that it does for you, help you to gain a more positive body-image. Mindfulness means being focused on your actions, which helps you to act with purpose. When you act with purpose, your thought processes become clearer to you.

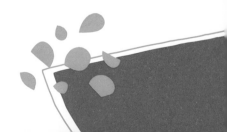

Use the space below to answer the following questions:

Do you regularly feel aware of your body and its needs?

....
....
....
....

How does the physical health of your body affect your frame of mind?

....
....
....
....

Reflect upon your body's journey; what it has been through, what it has survived and what it has accomplished. Write down what you are grateful for.

....
....
....
....

Use this space to write your own thoughts.

FEELING BETTER

Those who practise mindfulness experience greater feelings of well-being. Research shows that mindfulness can improve physical health, too, by helping to reduce high blood pressure and chronic pain. It also increases your ability to handle stressful situations and enhances your quality of sleep, enabling you to enjoy a deeper, more peaceful slumber.

Consider how you want mindfulness to improve your physical health and set yourself three health goals you would like to achieve.

1. ....

2. ....

3. ....

Why are these important to you?

....

....

....

What is your first step to achieving these goals?

....

....

....

Reflect upon your answers and write how these will benefit your day-to-day life.

....

....

....

Use this space to write your own thoughts.

AWARENESS IS THE GREATEST AGENT FOR CHANGE.

Eckhart Tolle

MAKE TODAY
A GOOD DAY

When you wake up in the morning, don't just jump out of bed to start the day; take time to be conscious of your body. Become aware of your thoughts, observe them as they come and go, letting them pass like clouds in the sky. Focus on your breathing. Listen to sounds around you and stretch your whole body to awaken your muscles. Make your bed mindfully to create a calm transition from sleep to the day ahead. When washing your face, notice how the water energizes you. It's also important to find a few minutes in your morning routine to sit calmly instead of rushing to start the day's activities. Focus on your breathing and visualize each breath filling your body with golden light. You will feel strengthened and ready for the new day.

A positive mantra is a motivating phrase that is repeated either out loud or in your head. Create some mantras to start off your day. For example, "Today is going to be a good day."

- ....
- ....
- ....
- ....
- ....
- ....
- ....
- ....

In the space below, explain what these mantras mean to you and how they will have a positive impact on your day.

....
....
....
....
....
....

Use this space to write your own thoughts.

RELEASE YOUR INNER CHILD

Every once in a while, pretend to be a child again.
Do you remember how curious you were then?
Mindfulness is seeing things with fresh eyes.
Bring back those childlike moments and find
a new way to behave mindfully. Children see
magic in everyday things: raindrops glistening
on leaves, stars twinkling in the sky, the slow but
sure progress of a snail making its way across the
garden. Look around and start seeing the world
through a child's eyes. It will brighten up your day!

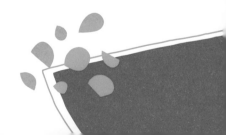

Choose one of your daily routines and approach it as if you are experiencing it for the very first time. Describe everything you notice, taking note of all five of your senses: touch, taste, smell, hearing and sight.

How did taking the time to appreciate every sensation feel?

In the space below, describe any "magic" moments you noticed that you miss every day.

Use this space to write your own thoughts.

THE PAST CANNOT BE CHANGED

WALK MINDFULLY

With daily practice, any activity you do can become a mindful activity. Take walking to the shops or to work, for example. As you walk, be aware of everything around you by engaging your five senses. Take deep breaths, listen to the sound of your footsteps, be aware of your body. Walking mindfully is your chance to slow down, appreciate your surroundings, let a feeling of calm wash over you. If you are out in the countryside, take notice of the blooming wildflowers and leaves on the trees, the sound of birdsong, the sight of animals grazing in the fields. If you are walking in a town or city, be aware of the aroma of coffee as you pass cafes, how doors feel if you go into a shop – are they made of wood, metal or glass? Notice the details – chimneys, rooftops, windows, architecture. Really look and see everything. You'll be surprised at how much you missed before!

Practise mindfulness while on a walk. In the space below, write down what you observed when you slowed down to appreciate your surroundings.

....

....

....

....

Describe the feelings you experienced while being more aware of your surroundings.

....

....

....

....

Reflect on how this mindfulness activity made you feel.

....

....

....

....

Use this space to write your own thoughts.

SLOW DOWN

Life demands so much of us these days, it's
really no wonder it often feels as though we are
continually racing against the clock. Slow down
by taking a deep breath, hold it for the count
of three, then slowly release it. Focus on each
of your senses, one by one, breathing deeply
as you do so to promote a sense of calm.

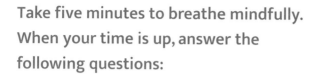

Take five minutes to breathe mindfully.
When your time is up, answer the
following questions:

What could you see?

....

What could you smell?

....

What could you hear?

....

What could you taste?

....

What could you feel?

....

Describe how you felt at the end of the activity.

....

....

....

Use this space to write your own thoughts.

WE TOO SHOULD
MAKE OURSELVES EMPTY,
THAT THE GREAT SOUL OF
THE UNIVERSE MAY FILL
US WITH ITS BREATH.

Laurence Binyon

DAILY PLEASURES

It is all too easy to let time pass without being particularly aware of it. An important part of mindfulness practice is to remember to feel joy every day and regard each day as your favourite. Notice the little pleasures – be mindful of the wind in your hair, how the sun feels on your skin, the fresh scent of newly laundered clothes or the sweetness of a fresh strawberry on your tongue. Take note of your daily rituals and instead of viewing them as boring chores that need to be completed, try to see them for what positives they bring to your life, whether it be meaning, learning or pleasure. If you change your mindset these "chores" will become enjoyable.

Take the opportunity to recognize some of the simple pleasures that you experienced today. Write what they were and how they made you feel.

- ....
- ....
- ....
- ....
- ....

In the space below, write three daily pleasures you could introduce to bring joy to your week.

1. ....
2. ....
3. ....

What else could help you to feel joy every day?

....

....

....

....

....

Use this space to write your own thoughts.

ALL ABOUT APPRECIATION

We're often so engrossed in our thoughts that we don't pause to appreciate our surroundings. This means interesting details are often overlooked. Encourage yourself to take note of the oft ignored. Your food is a good place to practise mindfulness because it engages all of your senses. You may usually notice how a meal tastes but try appreciating how enticing it looks, its colour palette or the textures. You could dedicate one day a week to focusing on just one sense while eating. For example, on Monday you could listen for the sound of your food while cooking, how it sizzles and pops, and how it crunches in your mouth. On Tuesday you could note the feel of your food, how the cool, hard vegetables become warm and soft as they cook. Really see the things you take for granted every day.

Using the following table, keep a food journal for a week. Describe the different sensations, textures, smells and tastes that you experience with each meal.

	Breakfast	Lunch	Dinner
MON			
TUE			
WED			
THU			
FRI			
SAT			
SUN			

Using the space below, reflect on how being mindful when eating has changed your eating habits.

....

....

Use this space to write your own thoughts.

EVERYONE'S JOURNEY IS DIFFERENT

DINNER DATE

Set aside time to enjoy your evening meal. Make this a part of your day where you can refocus and reconnect with yourself. Prepare your meals with love and focus. Notice the tantalizing textures of the ingredients at your fingertips. When you sit down to eat, make yourself engage in the experience by appreciating the smells, tastes and textures of the food. Eat slowly, savouring the taste of the food. Put your knife and fork down between each mouthful. Give the food your full attention, being grateful for the meal you are eating. Don't multitask by watching television, checking social media or chatting with friends online. Focus your attention on the act of eating. Your meals will taste better and you will feel better for it.

Cooking can be a great opportunity for you to practise mindfulness. Cook your favourite meal while being aware of all five of your senses.

Describe what you notice when paying more attention to each step of the recipe; for example, the noise of water boiling or how the skin of a vegetable felt in your hand.

touch

smell

sight

taste

sound

Use this space to write your own thoughts.

NO TIME LIKE
THE PRESENT

The past is gone and the future hasn't arrived yet.
You can't change what has happened and you
don't know what will come. Stop mulling over past
or future tasks and bring yourself back to the
here and now. The present is the place of power.
Now, in this moment, you can choose to be happy.

Embrace the present by answering the following questions:

What is good in your life right now?

- ....
- ....
- ....

What are you thankful for at this moment?

- ....
- ....
- ....

In the space below, write how and why you are choosing to be happy.

....

....

....

....

....

....

Use this space to write your own thoughts.

LIVING IN THE
MOMENT MEANS...
LIVING YOUR LIFE
CONSCIOUSLY, AWARE
THAT EACH MOMENT YOU
BREATHE IS A GIFT.

Oprah Winfrey

FOCUS ON THE TASK AT HAND

When you have a lot of things on your to-do list each task can feel overwhelming. It can be tempting to rush through the tasks just so that they are done, but in the long run it is more beneficial to slow down, dedicating time to each. Set aside blocks of time when you will complete your tasks and turn your electronic devices off, so you won't be interrupted or feel tempted to distract yourself by checking your social media. Work slowly, carefully and deliberately on one task at a time. Keep your mind on the present and focus on your actions. Try to enjoy whatever it is you are doing. You may notice that you find completing errands and life admin relaxing and fulfilling when you're not rushing to get them finished. Take the time at the end of each task to pause, take a breath and congratulate yourself before moving on to the next one.

Using the table below, schedule in some time for any tasks that have been neglected on your to-do list. Aim for at least one a day. Make sure your devices are off so you are not distracted.

	Task	How long the task should take	✓
MON			
TUE			
WED			
THU			
FRI			
SAT			
SUN			

Describe below how it feels to have finally achieved these tasks.

....

....

....

Use this space to write your own thoughts.

THE MUSIC OF MINDFULNESS

Listening to music is a good mindfulness exercise. Choose something soothing and turn off all other devices. Sit in a comfortable position in a space where you can minimize any distractions. Spend a few moments resting, focusing your attention on your breathing and immersing yourself in inhaling and exhaling. As you begin to listen to the music, focus on each note. Really take notice of the instruments, the dynamics and the tempo. Notice any feelings that the music conjures up for you and any sensations that occur in your body. If other thoughts creep into your head, gently bring your attention back to the music. Afterward, notice how much calmer you feel.

Create a list of some of your favourite pieces of calming music.

- ....
- ....
- ....
- ....

Choose one piece of music to listen to, then answer the following questions:

What feelings does the music conjure up for you?

....

....

Were you aware of any physical sensations in your body?

....

....

Describe how you felt by the end.

....

....

Use this space to write your own thoughts.

THERE IS LOVE AND BEAUTY ALL AROUND ME

MAKE PEACE WITH THE PAST

Part of mindfulness is accepting the things in life that you cannot change. While you may have gone through experiences that have challenged you, they ultimately made you the person you are today. There is always something to appreciate in life. Mindfulness encourages us to embrace acceptance and gratitude, which in turn allows us to appreciate what we already have. This makes us feel happier and our lives become more satisfying. Changing our mindset reduces negative thought processes and enables us to appreciate the good in our lives.

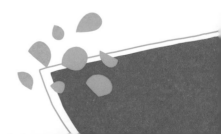

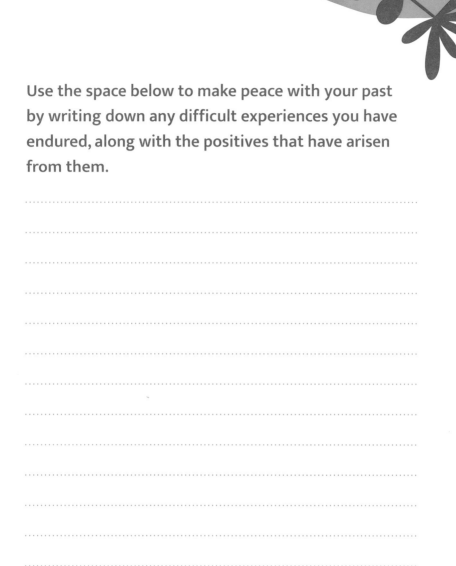

Use the space below to make peace with your past by writing down any difficult experiences you have endured, along with the positives that have arisen from them.

Use this space to write your own thoughts.

LISTEN TO
THE SILENCE

Close your eyes and listen for a minute to
the sounds around you. Don't do anything
else except listen. Being comfortable with
silence is essential to mindfulness practice.
Become aware of your thoughts. Focus
on your breathing. Be at one with the
silence and stillness. It will bring peace.

Sit down comfortably in a quiet place and concentrate on your body. Start from the top of your head and systematically scan your way down your body to your toes.

On the diagram, colour in the areas of your body you were most aware of.

Using a different colour, fill any areas you felt tension or pain.

Describe the sensations you felt.

....
....
....
....
....
....
....
....
....
....

Use this space to write your own thoughts.

LET US BE SILENT, THAT WE MAY HEAR THE WHISPER OF GOD.

Ralph Waldo Emerson

DAILY ROUTINES

Pick a routine daily activity that you normally do on autopilot and make it mindful. Let's say brushing your teeth, for instance, or getting dressed. Many of us do these activities barely noticing what we are doing. Pay attention to squeezing the toothpaste onto the brush, the contours of your mouth, what the toothpaste tastes like and how the brush feels against each tooth. Think about the clothes you put on. Are the colours muted or bright? Is the fabric soft or textured? How do the clothes make you feel? Take the opportunity to consider how you feel throughout the experience. When you pay close attention, you may pick up on things you haven't noticed or thought about before and you will find more enjoyment in these seemingly simple or mundane tasks.

Choose a routine daily activity to make mindful, taking note of all five of your senses while performing it. When you've finished the activity, fill in the Mind Map below with any small details and observations that you overlook every day.

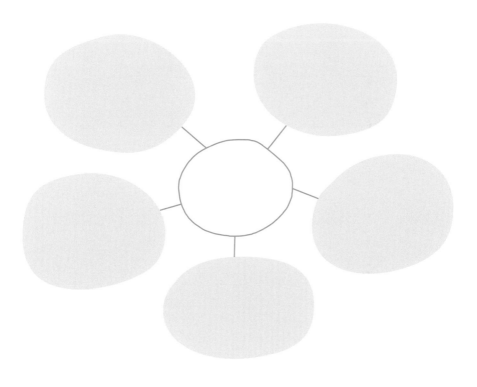

Describe how you felt during the activity.

....

....

....

Use this space to write your own thoughts.

TAKE TIME TO RECHARGE

Regardless of how many things you have to do, stop between tasks and breathe three complete breaths – this gives you an energy recharge to carry on with your day. Remember to allow yourself plenty of rest, too, especially when there are likely to be extra demands on your time. Set aside time every day to rest and recharge your batteries. A ten-minute walk or a powernap are great ways to help you to feel more relaxed, as well as increasing your productivity.

It's crucial to your well-being to give yourself time to recharge your energy. Take the time to check in with yourself by asking these questions:

How are you feeling at this moment?

....

....

....

....

Are you okay? If not, what can you do to change this?

....

....

....

....

Write down the names of people who will be there for you if you need support:

....

....

....

....

Use this space to write your own thoughts.

TO CARE FOR OTHERS, I MUST FIRST CARE FOR MYSELF

THOUGHTS ARE ONLY THOUGHTS

Remember that thoughts are just that – they are thoughts; they don't automatically represent reality. You can and should observe them without being subject to them. Unwanted, intrusive thoughts about your past or future can pop into your head without warning, at any time. This could happen because of any number of triggers, the important thing is to accept they exist but not ruminate upon them or let them hold any weight within your mind. When you practise mindfulness you will find you can enjoy the fullness of the moment, instead of focusing part of your attention on the past or the future.

Our thoughts often hold us back from being present in the moment. Use this space to write down and recognize what is currently going through your mind. Once you have acknowledged these thoughts, cross them out and move on.

Use this space to write your own thoughts.

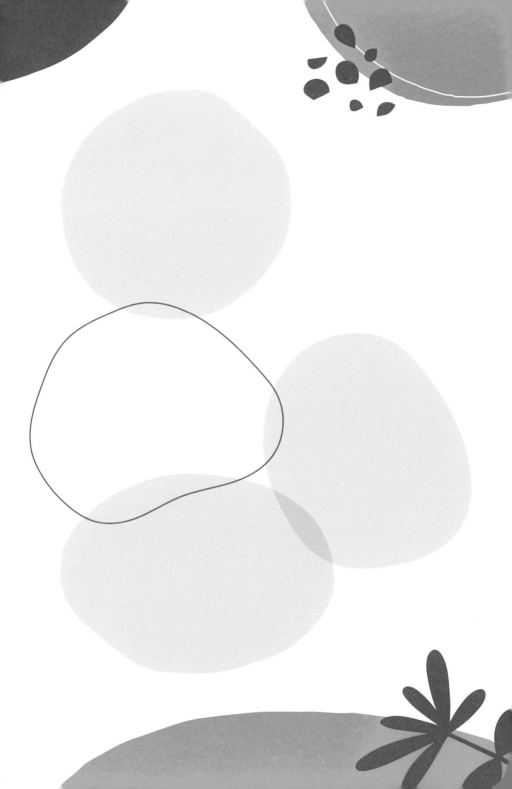

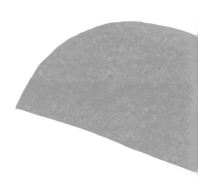

WONDERS OF WILDLIFE

Nature inspires. Its beauty and complexity has powerful appeal. When you're out in the country or on a train journey, look out for livestock grazing in the fields or perhaps wild animals in woodlands. In parks or gardens, notice birds flying overhead, or perching on branches. See how butterflies flit from flower to flower. Notice spiders busily spinning their webs; see the intricate patterns they create. Wildlife can make you smile and encourage your sense of wonder.

**Take some time out to experience nature.
Observe and record at least one of each of
the following:**

Something that made you smile.

....

....

Something that made you curious.

....

....

Something that filled you with a sense of awe.

....

....

Something that made you feel part of nature.

....

....

Something that made you feel hopeful.

....

....

Use this space to write your own thoughts.

AFTER ALL,
THE BEST THING
ONE CAN DO WHEN
IT'S RAINING IS
TO LET IT RAIN.

Henry Wadsworth Longfellow

THE BEAUTY OF NATURE

When you are out and about, look around: what colours do you see? Take in the hues of nature: the blue sky and white and grey clouds. If there are trees nearby, see their green or russet leaves. Taking time to notice and appreciate the colours of nature is a quick and pleasant way to be more mindful. If you have a garden, tune in to all your senses as you mow the lawn, dig the soil and tidy the flower beds – or just sit peacefully and enjoy your surroundings. If you don't have a garden, go to a park and notice the shrubs and flowers: their colours, their texture and any scent they may have. Notice the pebbles and grass. Really look at them and enjoy their special uniqueness. Pay attention to nature's beauty; it is all around us.

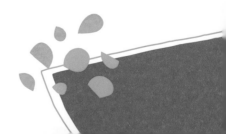

Find a space in nature and try sketching anything that you find particularly interesting. This doesn't have to be a masterpiece, just a snapshot of a moment. Use crayons or felt-tips to try to capture some of the colours you see.

Use this space to write your own thoughts.

TRY
SOMETHING NEW

It is easy to be mindful when you attempt to do something you have never done before. The way we behave when we are learning – moving slowly, taking care over our actions and considering each choice – is how we behave when we are being mindful. So to enjoy more moments of mindfulness, take up a new hobby or activity. It doesn't matter what it is: it could be learning Spanish or scuba diving, or going to a dancing class. Learning something new will also benefit your life in other ways outside of your mindfulness practice! It stimulates the mind and introduces new ideas into our lives. If you engage in a social hobby, you may even welcome new friends into your life. As you master your new skill you may have to work harder to remain mindful, but you will also feel positive emotions such as confidence and a sense of achievement.

Write a list of any hobbies you would like to take up or activities you would love to try in order to stimulate your mind.

- ....
- ....
- ....
- ....
- ....

What are your motivations for learning something new?

....

....

....

....

Describe how you feel about embarking on new experiences.

....

....

....

....

....

Use this space to write your own thoughts.

I AM
PRESENT
IN THIS
MOMENT

BRING YOURSELF BACK TO THE PRESENT

Three times a day, for one minute or so,
simply stop whatever it is that you're doing
and take notice of the feelings and thoughts
in your mind. Are multiple things whizzing
through your head or are you concentrating
on the present? If you realize that you are
distracted, guide your attention back to the
task in hand. Becoming more familiar with
your mind's habitual patterns can help you
to work with them much more skilfully.

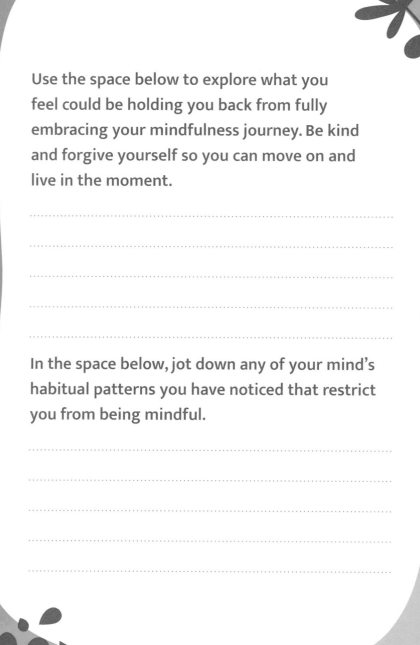

Use the space below to explore what you feel could be holding you back from fully embracing your mindfulness journey. Be kind and forgive yourself so you can move on and live in the moment.

....

....

....

....

....

In the space below, jot down any of your mind's habitual patterns you have noticed that restrict you from being mindful.

....

....

....

....

....

Use this space to write your own thoughts.

THERE'S NO NEED TO BE PERFECT

Immerse yourself in activities for the enjoyment they bring you, rather than with the goal of trying to achieve perfection. Dance because you love to move to music, not just because you are determined to improve your footwork; bake bread because you enjoy the comforting feeling of kneading dough and the aroma of the loaf while it is baking. Focus on the task in hand and enjoy it for the pleasure you feel when doing it. Imposing additional demands on yourself will detract from the joy of the activity. Good is good enough. No one can achieve perfection in every part of life, so pick and choose those areas where you feel content to be "just right". The results will be emotionally liberating.

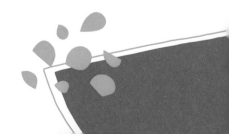

Write a list of what you love doing and what about it you enjoy the most.

- ....
- ....
- ....
- ....
- ....

Choose something from your list and make it a mindful experience. Describe how mindfulness enhanced the activity.

....

....

....

....

....

Write about a time when you have embraced the joy of the activity over the importance of achieving perfection.

....

....

....

....

....

Use this space to write your own thoughts.

IF WE WILL TAKE
THE GOOD WE FIND,
ASKING NO QUESTIONS,
WE SHALL HAVE
HEAPING MEASURES.

Ralph Waldo Emerson

NATURE'S BEAUTY

All flowers are beautiful, but how often do you really *see* them? The next time you see a flower, stop and take a closer look. Consider it carefully. Is it all one colour, or a combination of several? Look at its petals: are they large or small? Inhale the fragrance. Mindful practice can help you better appreciate beautiful objects and gifts of nature.

Find a flower that is easily accessible without removing it from its natural habitat. Draw it in the space below and surround it with as many adjectives describing it as you can.

What is your favourite thing about this flower?

....

....

Find another object from nature to appreciate and describe it in the space below.

....

....

Use this space to write your own thoughts.

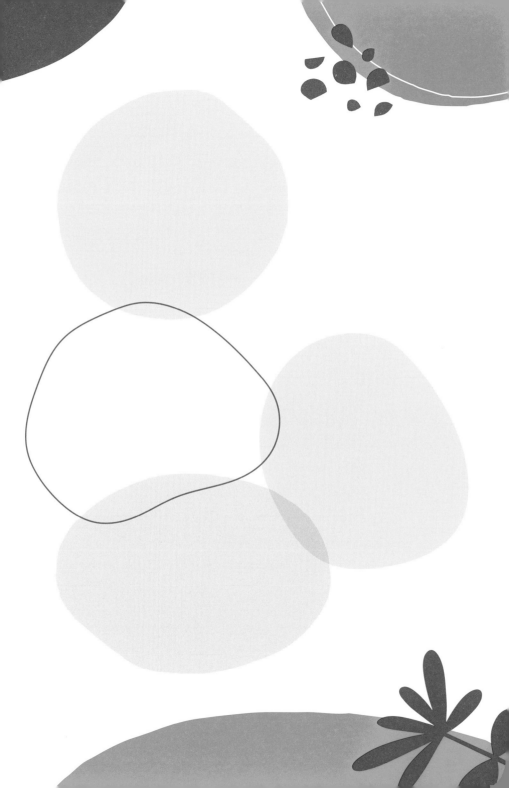

MOVE THAT BODY

Be aware and stay mindful of how your body reacts throughout the day. If you notice it feels tense in certain areas, perform movements that help to restore and refresh you. For example, if your shoulders are tense, stand up and shake out your arms to release them. Move as much as possible throughout the day, especially if your lifestyle is sedentary. If you are sitting most of the time, stand up and move around for a few minutes every hour or so. You could add extra movement to your day by standing instead of sitting on the bus or train, walking to the next bus stop on from your usual one or parking further away from your destination. Mindful movement helps boost your mood and your mental health.

Incorporate some of your favourite exercises that keep you in tune with your body into every day of your week. Complete the daily planner to keep you motivated.

	Activity
MON	
TUE	
WED	
THU	
FRI	
SAT	
SUN	

Use the space below to document how the experience has affected your mood and benefitted your physical health.

....

....

....

Use this space to write your own thoughts.

I AM
GOING TO
EMBRACE
TODAY

SWITCH OFF GADGETS

Nowadays it seems we are constantly bombarded with a non-stop stream of information from mobiles, computers and television. It can be overwhelming. Once in a while, turn off devices, put away any gadgets and give yourself a break from the lights and noise. Sit quietly and calmly. Be aware of your thoughts. Become comfortable with the peace and quiet. Try it first of all for 30 minutes. Then do it for a morning on your day off. Go for a walk, try a new recipe, do some embroidery, enjoying the feeling of peace it brings. As well as bringing calm, it will allow you to tap into the part of yourself that is often disconnected from the world around you.

Use the space below to answer the following questions:

How much time do you spend on devices a day? Set yourself a daily device time limit.

. . . .

. . . .

. . . .

Come up with a list of activities you could do instead of reaching for your phone.

- . . . .
- . . . .
- . . . .
- . . . .
- . . . .

Describe the positives reducing device time will have on your life.

. . . .

. . . .

. . . .

. . . .

Use this space to write your own thoughts.

AN OASIS OF CALM

Turn your home into a harmonious sanctuary
by making it as calm and peaceful as it can
possibly be. You could hang wind chimes at
a window or in a corner of a room to help
boost your home's natural energy. You could
also add a vase of fresh flowers or a thriving
green plant and some perfumed candles. Each
soothing element can be something to focus
your mindfulness practice on – note the gentle
sound of the wind chime or the beautiful bloom
of flowers as you move around your house.

Come up with six adjectives to describe how you would like your home to feel.

Use the space below to write down some ideas for making your home an oasis of calm.

....

....

....

....

Use this space to write your own thoughts.

PUT YOUR EAR DOWN CLOSE TO YOUR SOUL AND LISTEN HARD.

Anne Sexton

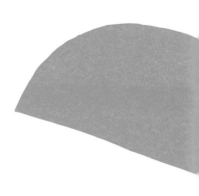

LOVE YOUR SPACE

A tidy home goes a long way to promoting the feeling of well-being. Clearing out items that you no longer need or that no longer bring you joy can help you to let go of the past and renew the energy of your space. Take it calmly and clear one room or area at a time. The past is behind you, let it go. Afterward, you'll feel amazing!

Pick a room a day to bring order and space to, using the following table to keep you motivated. If items are no longer used or bring you pleasure, give them away.

	Room/area	✓
MON		
TUE		
WED		
THU		
FRI		
SAT		
SUN		

In the space below, write down any new ways in which you feel inspired to use the space now that it has been cleared of extra items.

1. ....

2. ....

3. ....

Use this space to write your own thoughts.

MIX IT UP

Having a daily routine holds many benefits, but you can begin to feel stuck in a rut if you don't reform it occasionally. This can happen by sitting in the same spot for breakfast each morning, having the same thing to eat for lunch every day or always taking the same route to work. Consciously think about adding variety to your daily routine – whether it means taking a different route to the shops for a different view of your surroundings, or taking up a new hobby in your lunch break. Make a point of taking a day out just for you and do something that you like, or go and visit a new place. Varying routine tasks means we refresh our experience, which stops boredom setting in.

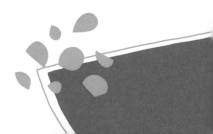

Using the table below, make one small change a day to your routine for a week. Write down one observation that excited, amazed or interested you, that you would otherwise not have experienced.

	Daily variation	Observations
MON		
TUE		
WED		
THU		
FRI		
SAT		
SUN		

Describe how varying your routine enhanced your day.

....

....

....

Use this space to write your own thoughts.

I AM LIVING MY LIFE WITH PURPOSE

EMBRACE
THE ELEMENTS

Do you try to avoid going out when the weather is bad? Does the rain or wind make you want to stay indoors? Next time you hear yourself complain about the cold or the wet, instead look for the unexpected joy in it. As the wind whips against your face, absorb its energy. A walk in the rain can add another dimension to your mindful behaviour as you can feel the raindrops on your skin, along with a heightened sense of sound as the rain falls to the ground around you. Listen to the wind blow through the tree branches and hear the leaves rustling. Enjoy the scent of wet earth after a rain shower. Nature is wonderful; take time to notice and appreciate it. The elements, whatever form they take, refresh and revitalize us.

**Use the space below to answer
the following questions:**

What sights, sounds and smells of the natural
world caught your attention today?

....

....

....

....

....

Write down three natural pleasures you experienced today.

1.
....

2.
....

3.
....

Reflect on a time you were able to look at something
familiar with fresh eyes. Describe the experience below.

....

....

....

....

....

Use this space to write your own thoughts.

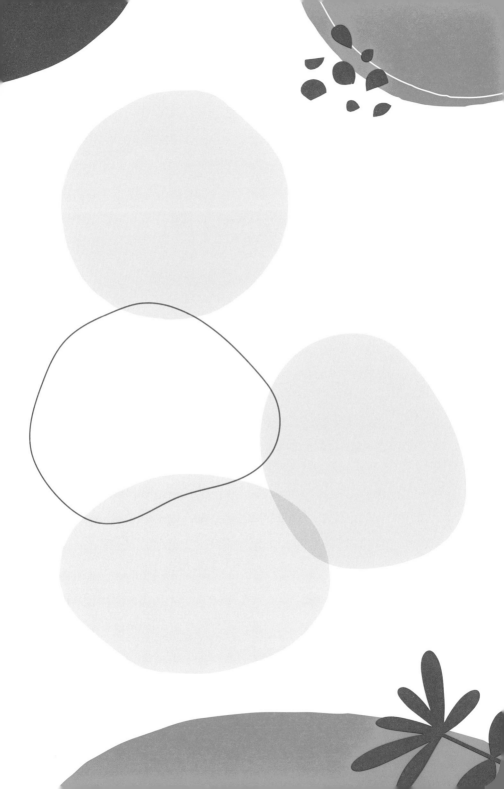

BE SELECTIVE

If you cram your days with activities, you will
find yourself rushing from one thing to the
next without stopping to think about what
you are doing. By filling up your days you are
unable to appreciate each task at hand and are
more likely to feel overwhelmed and stressed,
as it's impossible to complete everything to
the standard that you wish. Doing less means
you can fulfil those activities more mindfully,
more completely and with more concentration.
Maybe you think you are so busy that it is
not possible to do less? You can. Assess what
is important and let go of what isn't.

In the space below, answer the following questions:

What do you want from life?

....

....

....

What or who is most important to you?

....

....

....

What are your current top priorities and responsibilities in life?

....

....

....

Describe the first steps you would take towards embracing what is important to you in life.

....

....

....

Use this space to write your own thoughts.

IF PEOPLE JUST TOOK IT A DAY AT A TIME, THEY'D BE A LOT HAPPIER.

Richard Bachman

MANDALA MAGIC

Mandalas are spiritual and ritual symbols
consisting of geometric designs. One of their
uses is to aid meditation and mindfulness.
They have been used for thousands of years
in Buddhist and Hindu traditions. The process
of creating a mandala lets you tap into your
creativity and can help you restore inner peace.
Choose a design that appeals to you and let your
mind be absorbed by the patterns and colours.
Focusing on the shapes and symmetry of the
mandala brings your senses into the present
moment, while colouring it in is an excellent
mindfulness technique to relieve stress.

Colour the mandala, concentrating on the shapes and symmetry. Try to keep your mind focused on the activity. If your mind does wander, gently guide yourself back to the present.

In the space below, tap into your creativity by designing your own mandala.

Use this space to write your own thoughts.

BE GOOD TO YOURSELF

Perhaps you are well on the way to practising mindfulness daily now, but you are still slightly concerned that you cannot sustain it. Sometimes you may feel you are too busy to practise, or that when you do you can't stop your mind from wandering. Annoyance or frustration can naturally begin to creep in at these times. If this happens, actively choose to focus on forgiving yourself. Self-compassion will enable you to try again. You will get there in the end; have faith in yourself.

Create a list of relaxation techniques that could help you unwind.

- ....
- ....

- ....
- ....

Using the schedule below, add one element of self-care to your routine each day for a week for a more mindful week.

	Activity	✓
MON		
TUE		
WED		
THU		
FRI		
SAT		
SUN		

Describe any changes you noticed in yourself as a result of making at least one of these self-care practices a weekly habit.

....

....

Use this space to write your own thoughts.

I AM
MINDFUL OF
MY BODY AND
THE SPACE
AROUND ME

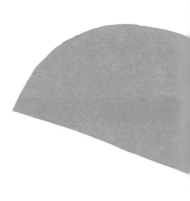

GREETINGS

The Sanskrit greeting "namaste" translates
as "I bow to you". To perform namaste, place
your hands together over your heart (at the
heart chakra), close your eyes and slightly
bow your head. Keep the phrase and its
meaning in mind when meeting other people.
It will remind you to listen mindfully and look
for the light in their words and actions.

**In the space below, answer
the following questions:**

What actions of others have positively
affected you in the past week?

....
....
....

What compliments have you received recently
and how have they made you feel?

....
....
....

What could you do to have a positive impact
on someone's life? Jot down some ideas for acts
of kindness you could perform this week.

....
....
....
....

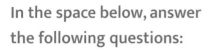

Use this space to write your own thoughts.

RISE AND SHINE

Getting up earlier in the morning to spend some focused time on yourself pays off. Really, it does! Try to get up at least half an hour before you usually do and luxuriate in being able to complete your morning routine mindfully and purposefully. Those extra minutes give you time to think, to focus on what you want – perhaps to do some yoga or stretching exercises. It will help you sustain a feeling of calm throughout the day.

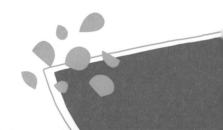

Create a morning routine to help start the day in a mindful way. Add in a healthy breakfast, some stretching exercises, and allow yourself plenty of time for reflection and to focus on what you want for the day ahead.

Time	Activity
__ . __ a.m.	
__ . __ a.m.	
__ . __ a.m.	
__ . __ a.m.	
__ . __ a.m.	
__ . __ a.m.	

Try a week of getting up 30 minutes earlier and in the space below describe how it helped you sustain a feeling of calm throughout the day.

....

....

....

....

....

Use this space to write your own thoughts.

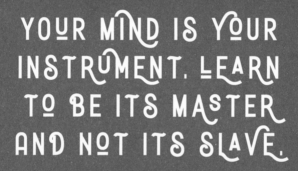

YOUR MIND IS YOUR INSTRUMENT. LEARN TO BE ITS MASTER AND NOT ITS SLAVE.

Remez Sasson

FINAL WORD

Congratulations for completing this mindfulness journal. Living mindfully can offer many rewards, such as improved mental health, increased focus and a positive outlook, so endeavour to use your newfound mindfulness skills to help guide you to a happier and healthier life. Continue to embrace acceptance and gratitude to appreciate what you have, enabling you to feel happier and more satisfied.

You may find during particularly busy or stressful times in your life it becomes hard to prioritize mindfulness. Try not to feel like this is a failing. One of the great things about mindfulness is that it is a skill that you can practise at any time and wherever you are; you do not always need to set aside a special time because you can learn to be mindful in any situation that you may find yourself in. Keep referring to your journal for motivation and inspiration and to see how far you have come along in your journey.

Happiness for Every Day Journal

Simple Tips and Guided Exercises
to Help You Find Joy

Paperback

ISBN: 978-1-80007-832-1

Positivity for Every Day Journal

Simple Tips and Guided
Exercises to Help You Look
on the Bright Side

Paperback

ISBN: 978-1-80007-833-8

Resilience for Every Day Journal

Simple Tips and Guided
Exercises to Help You Find
Your Inner Strength

Paperback

ISBN: 978-1-80007-834-5

Have you enjoyed this book?
If so, find us on Facebook at **Summersdale Publishers**, on Twitter at **@Summersdale** and on Instagram at **@summersdalebooks** and get in touch. We'd love to hear from you!

www.summersdale.com

IMAGE CREDITS